The Branscombe Projec

In 1996 we wrote:

In 1994 a group of people in Branscombe set up the Branscombe Project
(originally known as The Branscombe Millennium Project).
The idea is to investigate, write about and celebrate all aspects of
Branscombe, past and present. We want to know more about Branscombe's
history, about land-use and landscape, about crafts and industries, travel
and smuggling, about the history of the houses and of the people that have
lived in them. We want to find out about people's memories and
experiences of living and visiting Branscombe.

We hope that, eventually, everyone in the village will play some part in the project.
We want to establish an archive, have lectures and workshops, set
up nature and history trails, and mount exhibitions and entertainments.

Branscombe's ghosts has been one of our first projects, and we got so
many stories that we thought we should publish our findings. We hope that
this will be the first in a series of small village publications.

***

Now, thirteen years later, we're happy to report that the Project is still thriving and
that we've done a great many of the things that we set out to do, and a good many
more that we hadn't even thought of. Now, as then, the people we most want to
thank are those who live in the village. The Project is for them, about them, and
could only happen because of them!

We gratefully acknowledge funding from Grassroots, Rural Action,
Local Heritage Initiative and Awards for All.

We thank Nicole Segre with help with the design and production of this booklet.

*For further information on the Project, please contact Barbara Farquharson on
01297 680 448 or Joan Doern on 01297 680 359.*

Introduction

BRANSCOMBE has more than its fair share of ghosts – at least twenty-six apparitions at the last count, and that does not include various banging, tappings and singing. These ghosts – which take many different forms – appear to old inhabitants and incomers, to men and women, young and old.

It was Rita Saunders, who has lived at Branscombe all her life, who suggested that we collect these tales, and that we should hurry up before they were forgotten. She had stories to tell, and so did Wyn Clarke, Peggy and Sid Sweetland, Bill Carpenter, Mrs. E.N. Hughes – all people who have lived here all their lives. But then there were tales from people who had lived a long while in the village, and from relative newcomers. Amanda Hart, who lives at Hole Mill, not only collected earlier ghost stories that centred on the mill and the houses round about, but also told of her own encounters and those of visitors to the mill.

Mark was only five years old when he whispered to his mother about the 'nasty man' who was only visible from the waist up. And Mrs. Vickers' son was sixteen when he saw the Red Lady at York Cottage. Old and young see ghosts; though, I think it is true to say, school children today don't seem to recount stories.

Women are perhaps more pyschic than men, but they don't have the monopoly. Twenty men saw or heard things, compared to thirty-one women.

What of the content? Sometimes it's just a voice – usually a woman's voice, but it was a man's voice that said 'Lady, Lady...' below Shiela

Unwin's window. Sometimes the voice or voices are singing (two stories), wailing (two), chanting (one), humming (one), or chattering and laughing (one). Sometimes people hear sounds – banging (two), swishing (three), tapping (three), knocking (one), walking (two), dragging (one). Sometimes they feel something (four). Sometimes it's a poltergeist (three). And sometimes – quite often – it's an apparition (twenty-nine). Some of the apparitions, but not many, are traditional ghosts dressed in white (three). Many more are in period clothing (fifteen). Mainly the ghosts are human apparitions (twenty-seven), but sometimes they are dogs (two), or horses (two).

The earliest ghost we have found so far come from Berry Barton. The ghost of William Potbury was sighted in 1829/30; around this time, or perhaps a bit earlier, young Elijah Chick complained about the old lady in a red cloak, steeple-crowned hat and buckled shoes that 'comes in and looks in 'pon me'; and Orlando Hutchinson talks of a ghost 'with an old-fashioned head-dress and long pins stuck through her hair' in the mid nineteenth century. The fake smuggling ghost at the Old Vicarage in the Square dates between 1775 and 1830. The long Hole in the Wall poem about Church Living relates to events that occurred in the 1870's. Lilly Gush's father probably saw his ghost at the turn of the century; Elsie Chick's white horse was seen before the first world war; and Tom Lethbridge notes several sightings of the Red Lady at Hole Mill from the time of the first world war. But the ghosts have not gone away. The latest accounts are more or less of today or yesterday. And often, today, the people who recount the stories insist that they didn't believe in ghosts until they saw their apparition.

Where do they appear? There is a tight clustering around the middle of the village (see map p.32). We have not found any stories from places and houses that are further out – except at Berry Barton – although we are pretty sure that there must have been stories concerning some of the old houses like Edge Barton, Gays Farm, Weston etc. The stories run from Street to the Mason's Arms, up Vicarage Hill, and along to Greater Seaside. They extend inland to Hole Mill and Hole House. Some of the stories are about happenings on the road (five), or in a field or garden (eleven). Most are in houses (eighteen), and the houses are always old or, in the case of Lower House, on the site of an old house.

Most of the stories in this book were collected in the last few years. Joan Doern, Barbara Farquharson, Amanda Hart, Linda Hughes, and Shiela Unwin taped or wrote down peoples' accounts. Some came from written accounts, such as Orlando Hutchinson's *History of Sidmouth*, Mrs. Wolsley Harris's columns in *Pulman's Weekly News*, and Margaret Tomlinson's *Three Generations in the Honiton Lace Trade*.

There are two rather exceptional written sources. One is a long piece of doggerel verse, written in the late nineteenth century and entitled The Hole in the Wall. One 'spooky' evening in November 1995 this story was transformed into a short play by Jan Farquharson and was performed by some of the primary school children in the Village Hall. We have only included a short extract of this anonymous work since Margaret Rogers is going to publish an annotated version. The other source is the numerous writings by T.C. Lethbridge who lived at Hole House. He was an archaeologist and an ardent para-psychologist. We present a short account of this rather exceptional man on p.60.

The illustrations are by local artists, Carolyn Dixon and Angela Lambert.

Barbara Farquharson, May 1996

The Ghosts of Branscombe

Dedicated to the people of Branscombe, and most particularly to all
those who told their ghostly tales.

1

Berry (or Bury) Barton

The earliest written account of a ghost dates to the middle of the last century. It comes from Orlando Hutchinson's History of Sidmouth *(courtesy of Richard Eley of Sidmouth). It concerns a happening in a field known as Littlecombe 3 acres, at* **Berry Barton.**

9

The story numbers refer to the place-names on the map on page 32.

'A Stone Coffin was discovered in a field, over which there may originally have been a mound, but as the land had been from time immemorial under cultivation, nothing on that point can be ascertained now. About the beginning of the present century a loaded cart was passing through the field, when one of the wheels broke the cover of the coffin, which was only a little way below the surface of the groind. This led to examination, when the skull and some of the larger bones were taken out, and as it was reported, carried to the vicarage at Branscombe, and afterwards

buried in the churchyard. Twenty or thirty years after this, the tenant of *Bury Farm*, having a superstitious dread of the spot, wished that the coffin and its contents should be removed. It is said that a ghost, under the form of a lady with an old fashioned head-dress and long pins stuck in her hair, used to sit upon the stile in the dusk of the evening, so that the good people of the neighbourhood were much terrified, and would not on any account pass that way after dark. Some more of the bones were carried away, and then the subject in some degree dropped...'

85. A stone coffin was discovered in a field, over which there may originally have been a mound, but as the land has been [ploughed] time immemorial under cultivation nothing on that point can be ascertained now. About the beginning of the present century a loaded cart was passing through the field, when one of the wheels broke the cover of the coffin, which was only a little way beneath the surface of the ground. This led to an examination, when the skull and some of the larger bones were taken out, and as it was reported, carried to the Vicarage at Branscombe, and afterwards buried in the churchyard. Twenty or thirty years after this, the tenant of *Bury Farm*, having a superstitious dread of the spot, wished that the coffin and its contents should be entirely removed. It was that a ghost under the form of a lady with an old fashioned head-dress and long pins stuck through her hair, used to sit upon the stile in the dusk of the evening, so that the good people of the neighbourhood were much terrified, and would not on any account pass that way after dark. Some more of the bones were carried away, and then the subject in some degree dropped. The place may have been tampered with at other times, so that there could be but small hope that any thing more could be found. However, Mr. Heineken and myself, having heard these things, resolved that we would have a dig; and to this end we obtained leave of the owner of the land, Langdon, Esq. of Parrocks Lodge, Somerset. On Monday July 27. 1857, we drove over to the Sidmouth. The spot is indicated in the preceding small map under the heading, "EARTHWORKS CROSSDYKE, &c." The annexed plan is the locality on a larger scale. Mr. John Parrat the Sexton of Branscombe, shewed us the place.

| Coffin. 0.25? |
| Littlecombe |
| Three-acres. |

From History of Sidmouth *by Orlando Hutchinson*
Courtesy of Richard Eley of Sidmouth. (unpublished c. 1870)

Another ghost story from Berry Barton, recounted by Margaret Tomlinson in Three Generations in the Honiton Lace Trade, *p21:* There were persistent stories of an old lady in a red cloak, steeple-crowned hat and buckled shoes. The boy Elijah (Harriet Anne's younger brother) would not stay alone in bed, saying 'her comes and looks in 'pon me'. Betsy Croombs and a visiting Methodist preacher were among others who saw the old lady. A later tenant at Berry was said to have found a hoard of money built into the kitchen chimney near the spot where the lady used to vanish; after that she appeared no more.

Wyn Clark corroborates this story: They always used to say at Berry Barton that they used to see a little old lady up there with a red cloak on – my mother used to tell us stories about that.

Margaret Tomlinson in Three Generations in the Honiton Lace Trade *p.20*: (Harriet Anne Chick was born at Berry Barton in 1808 and died in 1875. She was the daughter of Abigail and Samuel Chick, first generation lace traders). In the summer of 1829, when Harriet Anne was still two months short of her twenty-first birthday, she was secretly married at Honiton Church to Lieutenant William Potbury, a naval officer in charge of the newly established coastguard station at Branscombe Mouth. It has long been suggested that her parents' opposition to the match may have been partly due to their deep resentment at the arrival of the coastguards in the village. All local people had enjoyed the benefits of smuggling, even if not actively engaged in it, and a 'preventative officer' would have been regarded as their natural enemy... Either way poor Harriet Anne never lived with her husband or returned home soon after the marriage, for almost immediately he was posted to a ship bound for the Carribean. Some time later, when the family at Berry was out, William Potbury was seen in a passage there by a servant girl called Betsy Croombs – or, some say, by one called Northcott. News was afterwards received that he had died in the West Indies on that very day. So convinced was the girl that she had seen him in the flesh that she is said to have asked the family on their return if a room should be prepared for him...

13

Berry Head

*Cliffy Gosling used to have a cliff garden below **Berry Head**. Peggy Sweetland, his daughter, recounts the following story.*

I was blackberrying on the cliffs above the church with my daughter and we both saw an invisible shape – like muslin – near a bush behind us. It was a place that my father often used to go to.

3

Margells

Margells is built on the site of a thirteenth century monastery. There have been many sightings of ghosts and other strange happenings.

Bill Carpenter, who lives two doors up from Margells told the following story: Mr Lee told me that he was just dropping off to sleep (in Margells) when he heard what he thought was his grandmother singing. He thought nothing of it.

He went away to war, came back, was just dropping off to sleep when he heard the singing again. He made a remark on the next day to his grandmother, who said it wasn't her singing, it must have been the 'singing monk'.

And Rita Saunders recounts: My uncle (Cox) and aunty lived there and he used to drive a steam roller. He brought a friend back to stay for the weekend, and when they went to bed they couldn't shut the stair-door. When they got up in the morning it just shut easy. And there was a very high mantlepiece (in the room nearest the road) and the clock very often used to fall off the mantelpiece. There was nobody there and it wouldn't break or anything ...
The visitors' book is full of different stories:

Mrs Pardoe from London 27.2.81: Margell's is built on the site of a 13th century Monastery. We think the two downstairs rooms are the remaining rooms of the original. The rest of the house is about 600 years old ...

The middle bedroom is haunted by a monk. If you move the bed (so that it is underneath) the window with the head touching the wall of the front room, the chanting of a monk can sometimes be heard as you drop off to sleep. A monk has been seen descending and ascending the stairs; this is a definite, authenticated story.

We had a psychic lady in who could only feel the presence of a young lad, aged about thirteen, with spiky blonde hair, in the middle bedroom.

At one o'clock one night we were standing by the kitchen sink happily talking when we heard a swishing sound right in front of us, then it occurred again. It was *not* wind or soot down the chimney. The ladies next door have the same noise in their upstairs room. Also during the night, in both large bedrooms we hear constant tapping, it seems to be on the floor. One night at 2 a.m. I heard chatter and laughter coming from somewhere in the house, I was in the front bedroom so it didn't come from next door and it most certainly was not in the street. We were the only two occupants of the house and my sister was asleep. It lasted for a few seconds only and was not repeated..

However, an unsigned note at the bottom of the page says:
This is nonsense, my brother-in-law who is well for known for being psychic stayed here and has told me that there is absolutely no ghost here at all! (so please take notice).

Betty Sutton, New Barn, Longfield, Kent. 21-28 Feb. 1981:
Ghostly Fred has not actually appeared, but his presence has been well and truly felt. If he likes you, he may sing to you, but only in the middle bedroom, or screen room as it is called. He does come downstairs, and if he does, he will 'swish' by you as he passes the fire-place, in which he baked his bread. Also he will tap at night, or walk on the floor above you ... These are true facts. I should know. I have been coming past this house for just over 30 years, and when I was about nineteen I was to have married the

grandson of the original elderly occupants, who were born and died in this house. Sadly this was not to be, and we are now both grown up and leading separate lives ... I can assure you that the Ghost is a very friendly Monk, who will do you no harm.

May/June 1978: Ghost seen walking about the bedrooms at 1–2.30 a.m. Tappings on walls and footsteps. He often makes benidictine (sic) in the sink. We can tell by two mistakes he makes, one he leaves the tap on, and two you can sometimes smell it.

16 Nov. 1981: With two children. On (the) first night a ghostly wail outside the window, definitely children, but could

see nothing. Strange shadows dancing on ceiling and gusts of cold air. Henry, aged two, kept running along the landing in his nightshirt, chatting and laughing with non-existent companions.

4

Pitt Farm To Blue Ball

Rita Saunders: Between Pitt farm and Blue Ball there was somebody who died. My mother used to say about a ghost called Jo Minify. My mother never saw him.

5

Grapevine

Wyn Clarke: If my mother was ill in the bedroom upstairs she saw this little lady in red come in and look on her. .... And mother would say 'Why troubliest thou me?' Mother used to speak to her and then it would float away.

And when I was expecting my child ... we were living in the top house then (Grapevine)... I was laid facing the window and I don't know what made me half-turn but I sort of felt a presence and as I half-turned it was like a Welsh woman with a big hat looking in over on me. As I turned she flitted away ... She was in black...

They were not frightening..

6
Windy Cott

Rita Saunders: My sister and Wyn's sister, they used to hear music playing in there but there was nobody living there ...

7

Coombe Cot

Dian Bird: We met a couple from Wales who used to have Doreen Hayes' cottage and she told us experiences of a presence there. When they went to bed — husband and wife — and the husband went downstairs, to spend a penny or whatever, she had this feeling that there was someone else in bed with her being quite amorous. This happened about two or three times ... She saw a shape of a gentleman — wearing ruffles.

8

Church Living

Dinah Denning: It was early morning in the spring of 1970. We were at home in Church Living. Church Living belongs to the National Trust and is reputedly one of the oldest inhabited homes in Devon.

My husband Ron and I were asleep in the bedroom at the left end of the house, looking towards the church. We both woke up because our bed was shaking violently. Then there was a loud knocking at the bedroom door. Ron thought my guests wanted to see me so I put on my dressing gown and opened the door. No-one was there. I then realised I hadn't any guests staying at the farm that night. Our daughter Rachel wasn't at home either, because she was sleeping the night at her grandparents.

We then went around the house together and walked outside. Everything was in order. The morning was extraordinarily calm and still. We looked at each other in amazement. We both knew what we had felt and heard. Was someone trying to contact us? We lived in the house for a further five years and in that time there were no more rude awakenings.

We were told that there was a secret passage under the church and there were places in our hallway that were quite hollow. We never investigated, we never had time.

I can remember it as if it were yesterday. The strange thing was I wasn't frightened, and neither was Ron. The bed was really shaking. I shall never forget that till my dying day. And definitely it wasn't a tap, it was boom, boom, boom! Dramatic.

Paul and Lalage Glaister : We lived in Branscombe for seven years (1976-1982). During that time we were in Church Living and never actively met any ghosts. With the exception of one time I remember. Lalage will remember this too. We knocked a window in the back of Church Living where the living room is now. At the back there was a raised bank where they used to grow early potatoes. And once, both Lalage and I remember looking out through that window and seeing quite definitely someone walking along the bank. Coming along from where Ron and Jo were (the house to the west of Church Living), going along and just evaporating.But otherwise the fact remains that all the time we were there there were nothing but benevolent feelings there. Even our dogs and cats were entirely at home. There was this feeling of well being and peace. We tried to find ghosts there. We spent ages trundling up and down the garden of Church Living with coat hangers in our hands trying to divine where the gap, the tunnel, was underneath. Unfortunately, we never found it. But on that one instance we definitely saw a figure walking purposefully along the back. We all felt, when we were going around the garden, a presence, someone waiting to be found. We never managed to find them but maybe we have to work on the basis that metal coat hangers don't make the best divining rods.

Church Living: The Hole in the Wall

A long poem entitled The Hole in the Wall *was given to Phoebe Spencer by Miss Freeman in 1950. Miss Freeman came to Branscombe in 1894, aged fourteen, and worked as a servant for the Rev. Swansborough. She still remembered Will Abbott. Will was Betty Rawson's grandfather.*

The poem recounts the story of how a passage was found in the roadside wall of Church Living. Will Abbott explored it and found a great many helmets. He removed one, and a distressed ghost materialised. So the helmet was hastily thrown back down the passage and the Rev. Swansborough blocked the hole...

The Introduction to the poem* suggests a possible origin of the helmet. In 1685 the Duke of Monmouth (illegitimate son of Charles II) landed in Lyme Regis and raised the flag of rebellion in the Protestant cause. Four hundred East Devon men, including, perhaps, some from Branscombe, followed him to Sedgemoor. Defeated in battle they fled home pursued by the wrath and terror of Judge Jeffries. And, once they got home, they hid their arms and uniforms.

*The Introduction was written by Margaret Rogers who is going to publish an annotated version of the poem.

But anon it appear'd that a mystical being
Of a kind we are not in the habit of seeing,—
A member of some subterranean society,—
Did not think that bold Will had behaved with propriety.
In the yard of Church Living a very strange sight
Was seen by the village-folk often at night,
A hitherto-never-beheld apparition,
Like a bundle of straw in a state of ignition,
Which sway'd to and fro with a slow restless motion,
As a boat with the ebb and the flow of the ocean.
Seen by *us*, such a weird *oscillation* might bring
Reminiscence, perhaps, of a person call'd *Swing*,
Well, or rather, *ill* known, as the Genius of arson,
Who 'gainst threshing-machines carried igneous wars on.
This terrible sight put the folks in a fright,
As it seem'd to *demonstrate* that all was not right;
Especially those in the farm-house who dwelt,
With it close to their doors, much disquietude felt,
And took it to heart to be so incommoded
By a portent, which certainly nothing good boded;
And often debated what course was most proper
To put on this dreadful annoyance a stopper.

In order this troublesome matter to settle,
Will Abbott surrender'd the head-piece of metal:
By the parson's advice, it was thrown, like a bowl,
With a strong underhand pitch, far into the hole,
Which was then closed with stones and cement very neatly—
Expedients which answer'd the purpose completely;
For the igneous spectre at once ceased from giving
Disturbance and fright to the folks of Church Living.

Extract from: The Hole in the Wall. (*Anon*)

THE HOLE IN THE WALL

"I ain't a bit fear'd going into that hole......" Bet..

"....at the snug **Fountain Head**"

"s'l I will!"
"DONE"

this terrible sight put the folk in a **fright**!

....a hither-to-never beheld **apparition**....

...like a bundle of straw in a state of ignition...

.5/- you don't Will Abbott! "

25

by the parsons advice,
Will Abbott surrender'd
the head piece of metal....
it was thrown, like a bowl
with strong underhand pitch
far into the hole....

Angela Lambert 96

Village Hall

T.C. Lethbridge Ghost & Divining Rod, *p.55:* My wife went for a sale of work in Branscombe village hall. She noticed Mrs. A. come into the hall with a little brown mongrel dog on a lead. She noticed particularly because there was another dog, a miniature collie, in the room at the time and she hoped that they would not fight. Mrs. A. passed out of sight with her dog, round a corner in the hall. My wife noticed that both woman and dog looked happy and enjoying themselves. After a time Mrs. A. went out again without her dog. My wife saw this and thought, 'Oh dear, she has left her dog tied up somewhere and has forgotten it'. She went to look hastily, but there was no dog anywhere.

Mrs. A. used to live in a house ... at Littlecombe ... her sister-in-law works for us here at Hole. The next time the sister-in-law arrived here, my wife asked her what kind of dog Mrs. A. had.' She has no dog now,' was the reply. 'But her husband had one, which was very devoted to him, but that is dead too. Her dog died more than five years ago. She was very fond of it.' The description of the brown mongrel was that of the dog which had died more than five years previously.

In Enid Temple-Cotton's version of this story, the lady was called Mrs. Smith and the dog was a jack russell!

10

Mill Farm

Shiela Unwin: It was about ten years ago. It was in the afternoon and I went down to see Dinah Denning. I parked the car before you get to the little stream. As I was about to get out, somebody came out of her kitchen and went into the open door of the barn (the mill room). I crossed over the stream and I put my head in the barn and shouted and nobody came out except the cat. I though, 'Well, that's

odd, nobody's there'. So I knocked on the door. Dinah came out at once, so I said, 'Well, that's funny, who went into the barn?'. And she said there wasn't anybody. From a distance the person had a very long black skirt ... I seem to remember she had a white blouse, and maybe an apron.

27

Phoebe Spencer (May 1st 1989): I just had this feeling that the field at the end of Mill Lane was slightly haunted. I was once there when my sister was going to the farm to speak. It was when the Dowells were there, I think. I stopped the car at the end of Mill Lane and she got out and went to the house and as she came back and she was unlatching the gate I heard a very urgent whisper. I couldn't hear the words but it was very, very anxious. I look round, there was nobody there. When my sister came, I said, 'What were you whispering?' and she said, 'Nothing', and I realised I couldn't possibly have heard her, she was too far away. ...Somebody else told me about that lane – they'd seen somebody riding a horse ...

10

Mill Farm...again

Mrs. Paget (July 17th 1996): When I first came here. I kept hearing about the ghost stories and the smuggling etc. There was a story going around that two of the ladies that lived in the village came back from Sidmouth with their donkey and cart. They'd been shopping. And they saw a lady riding a white or a grey horse somewhere in front of them. So they hurried along to try and catch her up, and as they turned the corner there was nobody to be seen.* So consequently we heard this story about the white or grey horse and I went to bed one night feeling very tired. I hadn't long moved in, and I must have woken about three o'clock in the morning, still desperately tired. But wondering why I had woken up, you see. Anyway, all of a sudden I heard this horse, horses hooves, going along the back lane to Ronnie's farm. I thought, 'well it must be a horse, I can hear the hooves'. But I was still too lazy or tired to get out of bed. But I knew that it couldn't get further than Ronnie's place. It couldn't get through because they've got the gates etc. Anyhow after awhile I could hear it coming back so by then I'd woken up, so I got out of bed, looked out the window. It was quite a warm night. And this white or grey horse was coming up the lane. So I thought well, it's not a joke you know. It's not a ghost, it's somebody's horse. I didn't quite know what to do about it. But, of course, the next day, I was telling one or two of the ladies about it, and they felt as if there had been a ghost, you know, coming up the lane

* See p. 58.

11

Culverwell

Jenny Newton: There were seven holly trees that were supposed to be seven sisters. And there was supposed to be a ghost ...

12

Wobble

Shiela Unwin: I was lying in bed one beautiful sunny morning with the window open and I must have just woken up. It must have been six or seven o'clock and I distinctly heard a voice saying 'Lady...'. A man's voice. So I looked out the window and there wasn't anybody there. And then it struck me I'd just heard a voice from the past and he might have been calling an animal – a cat or a dog, or a pony..

Barnell

Wyn Clarke: My sister and I used to work at Barnell for the Miss Sumers; she used to do the cleaning and I did the cooking. So one day they went out, and my sister said to me, 'I'll take you round while there's nobody about, show you the house, see.' Up we goes, up the big flight of stairs, has a look around. On the first landing, coming down from upstairs, we stopped and looked over the railings down into the big entrance hall. We hadn't been there two minutes when we heard these little footsteps walking across the hall. 'My god', I said, 'they've come back'. But they hadn't and this was, we thinks, one of the Miss Tuckers that used to live there. We thought it was their ghost coming back. I said, 'I can't stay here', and I dashed down the stairs and went outside.

My sister said, 'Well, I knew it was haunted': she used to clean the stairs, and one day, on the last flight, up the top of the building, she felt something brush against her — someone's skirt caught her as she went to go up the stairs.

We didn't say anything because you don't know whether they'd believe you or not ... we were only the servants ...

Barnell...again

Sid Sweetland: When I used to keep the car over at the garage (down by the Village Hall) and I used to go out at all sorts of times in the morning and I walked past Barnell's bottom gate and you could go past a dozen times and nothing, but just sometimes, early in the morning, round three o'clock, you'd get a cold shiver...

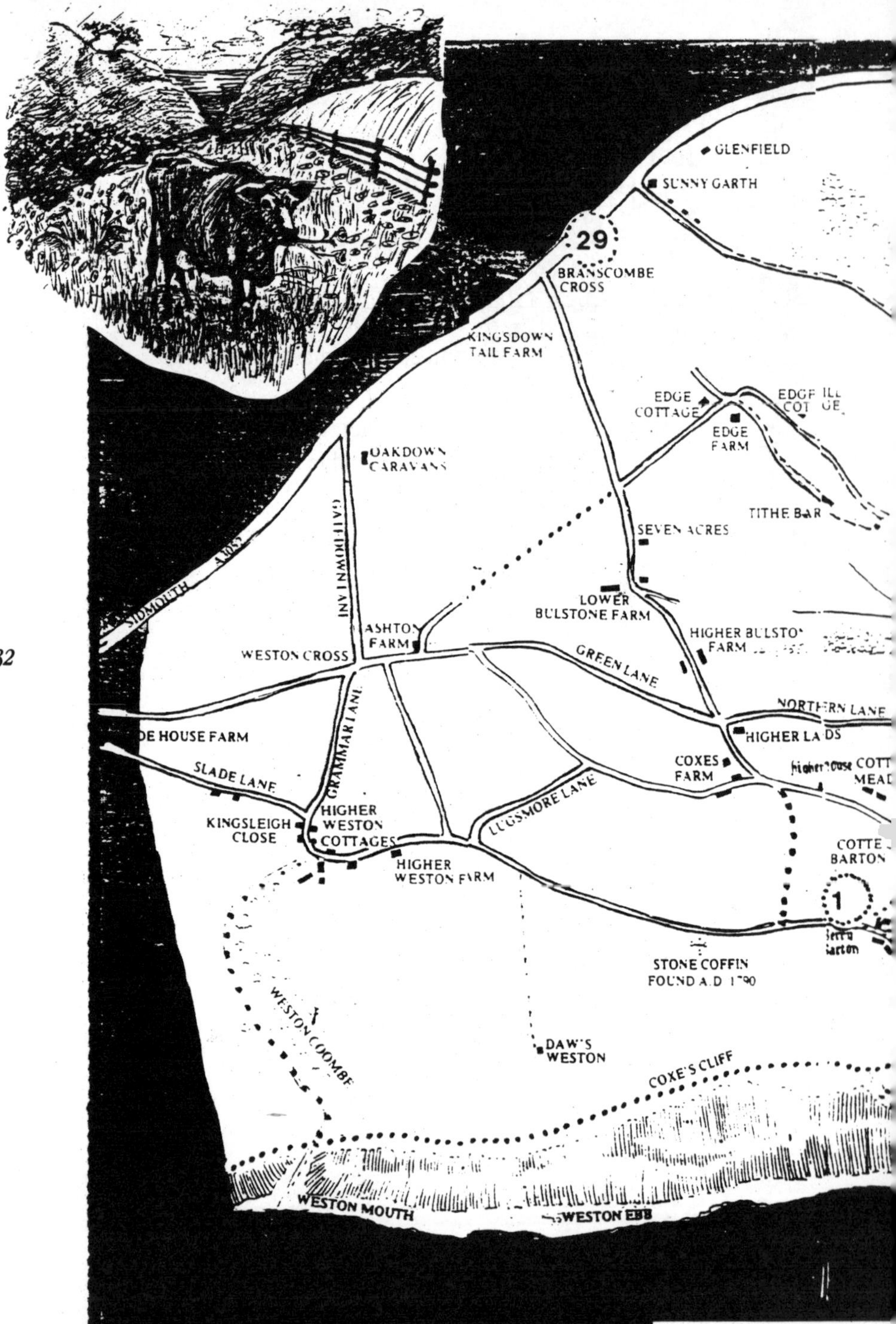

GLENFIELD

SUNNY GARTH

29
BRANSCOMBE
CROSS

KINGSDOWN
TAIL FARM

EDGE
COTTAGE

EDGE HILL
COTTAGE

EDGE
FARM

TITHE BAR

OAKDOWN
CARAVANS

SEVEN ACRES

LOWER
BULSTONE FARM

HIGHER BULSTONE
FARM

ASHTON
FARM

WESTON CROSS

GREEN LANE

NORTHERN LANE

DE HOUSE FARM

HIGHER LANDS

SLADE LANE

COXES
FARM

higher house COTTAGE
MEAD

KINGSLEIGH
CLOSE

HIGHER
WESTON
COTTAGES

LUGSMORE LANE

COTTE
BARTON

HIGHER
WESTON FARM

1

Berry
Barton

STONE COFFIN
FOUND A.D 1790

WESTON COOMBE

DAW'S
WESTON

COXE'S CLIFF

WESTON MOUTH

WESTON EBB

SIDMOUTH ROAD

GATCOMBE LANE

GRAMMAR LANE

BRAN

14

Hole Mill

There are many ghost stories that occur in and around Hole Mill.

Amanda Hart has collected some of them together. The first is about a ghost that she saw herself:

I will never know whether I saw a real ghost that early summer fifteen years ago ... There was only me there with my baby, so I had no witness to agree or deny what I saw.

I was in the bedroom that had once been the top floor of the watermill. There is a small window there, that would have been above the wheel, from which you could look out into the garden and up the drive. The drive is quite long and slopes uphill before flattening out about fifty yards from where I was. At the time we had a big, heavy, old garden roller which we had parked at the side of the drive on the beginning of the flat bit. When I looked out of the window that day I was really surprised to see an old lady sitting on the roller eating sandwiches. ... She did not appear robust enough to have walked from the village, and she certainly didn't live close by ... Picnicking in someone else's garden is a strange thing to do – our drive doesn't look like the continuation of the lane. Most importantly, her whole appearance was out of place – she was of slight build with light grey hair pulled back in a low bun and she was wearing a long dark skirt and a white blouse with cuffs and a high collar.

I finished what I was doing – changing a nappy, I think – and when I looked out of the window again she had vanished. Was she a ghost?

I spoke recently to Susan Restorick whose parents owned Hole Mill before us. She said the description of my old lady sounded like that of Mrs Vickers who used to live in York Cottage but died before we moved to Branscombe.

The rest are stories told to her:

Susan (Restorick) recounted a spooky tale about Halloween night in 1971: Susan, her young daughter, and her sister were in Hole Mill on their own. They had been teasing the little girl that on Halloween at midnight if you looked into a mirror you would see the face of the person you would marry. Exactly at twelve o'clock that night there was a crash and the mirror in the bathroom smashed into the washbasin.

Amanda's son, Simon, aged eight, was asleep in one of the bedrooms. He heard the door opening and the window banging, and then something pushed against him on the bed. He felt down the bed. There was nothing. Then it stopped – and then it started again. He ran to his mother's bedroom ...

This story tallies with an account written by a visitor, J. Pleace, on Sept. 5th, 1994: I was asleep in a bed next to the door. I awoke with the covers pulled back and lay there for awhile thinking about getting a drink when I felt 'somebody' was watching me.

I didn't open my eyes and lay there trying to convince myself I was being stupid when 'it' or 'they' moved at me. I shot under the covers next to my partner who was asleep and the feeling passed.

I didn't see anything and at no time was the room cold, in fact I was hot.

Another visitor said that he had heard a ghost 'humming rhythmically – 'like an old lady doing her darning'– in the kitchen when he was washing his coffee cup. He felt very comfortable with her presence.

A letter from another visitor to Hole Mill:

> *Dear Amanda,*
> *I have not forgotten that you asked me to send you a few words on the "hauntings" at Hole Mill ...*
> *I heard the loudest and completely inexplicable noise first of all in the bedroom (vacant) next to that of mine and Janet Simpson. There was a very loud banging, almost thunderingly loud on the wall between the two rooms. It sounded as though it was on wood, hollow wood, rather like the back of a wardrobe. And the sound of something very heavy indeed being dragged across the floor – but the floor was carpeted! Janet and I both looked into the room several times while this was happening, but saw no one, and then silence.*
> *Similar noises were heard directly over my bed, at the head – dragging and banging. The two sources of sound of banging were distinct and did not take place at the same time. We heard them the first three nights, but not on Saturday, nor Sunday. They were really very loud.*
>
> *Yours sincerely,*
>
> *Sonia Stanhope Wyrill*

Tom Lethbridge wrote of an encounter at Hole Mill in Ghost & Divining Rod *(pp.31-33):*

Feb. 22nd 1959: I was standing beneath a large sycamore tree on a hillside ... above Hole Mill ... At my feet a streamlet ran round the foot of the tree and vanished into the slope of the hill ... The Mill was perhaps sixty yards away. From this point I observed the figure of a woman, in clothes about forty years out of date, beside the Mill ... I had seen what is known as a ghost ...

Mrs. N. (Norris), who owned the Mill in 1959, told us that a week or two before I saw my ghost, she had seen another. This was the figure of a man in a tall hat, who was standing near the point where I stood. She had seen this on a misty day. Other people remark on the pleasant atmosphere of the spot. It seems then that the emotion that impressed these ghosts on this ... naiad-field was a pleasant one.

In Ghost and Ghoul *Lethbridge elaborates on this story. Overleaf is his drawing of the figure that he saw:*
(He sees Mrs Norris and) a second figure appearing behind her. She looked about sixty-five to seventy years old, was taller than Mrs N. and rather slight. Her face appeared to be rather dark, or tanned, and she had a pointed chin.

She was dressed in a dark tweed coat and skirt and something which looked like a light grey cardigan ... beneath her coat. Her skirt was long. She had a flat-crowned and wide-brimmed round hat on her head. The hat was black and had a wreath of white flowers round the bottom of the crown....

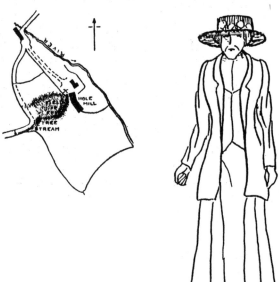

From T.C. Lethbridge
Ghost and Ghoul.
(Routledge & Keegan Paul 1961)

15

Hole House

Tom Lethbridge, who lived at Hole House, believed in time warps. He wrote an account of a time-warp happening at Hole House in Ghost & Divining Rod *pp.50/51, and in* A Step in the Dark:

When we came to Hole House in the late fifties, the daughter of the former owner of Hole House came to see the place again ... The woman told my mother-in-law that her mother had often seen a ghost about forty years earlier (about the time of the 1914-18 war). It was a little old woman with white hair and a red coat. She had been seen so often that she was known to all the old-timers of Branscombe.

Well, we think we know perfectly well who the red lady was. She was Mrs. Norris ... who lived down below us at Hole Mill. Mrs. Norris took to dropping in on Hole House unannounced. The first intimation we would have that she was in the house was for one or other of us to come into the hall at dusk and find a little figure, half-seen in the corner, taking off a pair of seaboots and putting on some slippers ... In cold winter weather she invariably wore a long cherry-red coat. She had no hat, had a shock of curly, white hair and usually carried a large 'otter-hunter's' thumbstick. Mrs. Norris had been a student of the magic arts and she believed that she could leave her human body and fly around visiting the houses of her friends.

The 'real' Mrs. Norris never appeared in Hole House before 1958; the ghost of the red lady was seen frequently around the years 1911-18 or perhaps even earlier. Tom Lethbridge was convinced that the little red lady was a projection back in time of Mrs. Norris.

Ron Hibbard reported in the Branscombe Quarterly *of Spring 1977:*

Archie Bromfield who was born at Hole Mill in 1901, told me the other day that his mother was a Miss Irish before she married Archie's father and that she used to live at Hole House. She and other members of her family used regularly to see the ghost of a little old lady in a red coat, usually to be seen sitting on a cider cask when they were sent out to draw another jug.

In the 1950s at least four people claim to have seen the ghost of a white dog in the lane outside Hole house. Tom Lethbridge wrote in Witches: Investigating an Ancient Religion *(p.68):*

When we had just moved in here, three years ago, my wife noticed a large white dog standing at the gate and looking in, in a friendly manner. It was a collie, with streaks of yellow on its head and neck. I asked my tenant, who farms the surrounding land, whose dog it was and he replied that there was no dog like that for miles around. We have no dog. We have not seen the white dog again.

Not just Hole House and Hole Mill but most of the cottages in Hole Bottom have more than their fair share of ghosts.

16

Bottom Cottage

John Kerswell as told to Angela Lambert: One fine summer morning in 1976, around 7.30 a.m., John Kerswell was dressing for work and, at the same time, glancing out of the bedroom window. Whilst doing up his tie his attention was suddenly drawn to a tall figure walking away across the bridge towards Lancaster

41

and York cottages. It was an unusual occurrence to see strangers walking around these parts any time, let alone 7.30 in the morning and wearing fancy dress.

The female figure was dressed in a long one piece gown or cloak which may have had a hood. It was strange, John recalled, not noticing her hair or head as the detail he was drawn to was how her heels kicked up the hem of her gown as it trailed on the ground as she walked. He watched in fascination as she quite literally disappeared as she passed behind a large lilac tree. He expected her to reappear a little further on where the hedge height was much lower and would have allowed a clear view of anyone continuing along the lane towards Hole Mill.

This puzzling manifestation was compounded by the fact that John's labrador, Tara, was sniffing about on the bridge at the same time as the lady passed by but was apparently oblivious to her or unconcerned. Tara always responded to passers-by in an excitable, often intimidating manner, quite the opposite of what happened that particular morning.

This was the one and only sighting by John Kerswell of the Grey Lady, but she left a lasting impression on him.

Lancaster Cottage – and the Grey Lady again...

These stories are told by Amanda Hart:

Alan Hearn owns Lancaster Cottage, now called The Linhay. It is on the opposite side of the bridge from John Kerswell's house. About eight years ago Alan woke up at about 3 a.m. – sober he asked me to stress – and in a dark corner of his bedroom he saw a figure radiating light. She was a tall woman standing about seven feet high wearing a long dove grey cloak and smiling benignly. He woke his wife, Angela, to show her and as she awoke the ghost disappeared. He mentioned the sighting of a lady to John Kerswell the next day and before he had time to describe her John immediately asked if she was a tall lady with a grey cloak! They had never discussed John's sighting of the grey lady at any time before.

A former owner of Lancaster Cottage, Barbara Sealey, who is quite elderly and whose memory is not so clear, says that she remembers a visitor saying that she had seen a figure of a woman upstairs – she thinks on the minstrel gallery. The figure was wearing a red dress.

York Cottage – and the Grey Lady again...

Frank Snelson recounts that about twelve years ago he saw a lady in grey on his landing ...

Joan Doern recounts a story told her by Mrs Vickers in the Spring of 1977:

In the 1970s the Vickers lived at York cottage. The first incident at the cottage which was unusual was in late winter. They had guests and had been sitting in front of the sitting room fire for several hours chatting when suddenly their two young golden Labradors started to growl and the hair on their backs stood up. Then suddenly they both launched themselves at the fire and had to be dragged outside to stop them jumping into the fireplace, fire and all. As the fire had been burning strongly for several hours, they all thought it unlikely that there was an animal or bird in the chimney.

Then, during Easter, Mrs Vickers was woken in the night by someone shaking her and trying to push her out of bed (her husband slept in another bed at the other end of the room). She woke to find a very small lady dressed in dark red standing by her bed. She then just disappeared.

The following night she was again woken, this time feeling that she was being throttled. Again it was the lady in red who then disappeared. The strangest part was that she had no sense of fear.

The next morning she told her husband, an executive with Thames Television. He drew a sketch of her description of the red lady and took it to the costume department at Thames. They felt they could date her, from the sketch, to a ten year period in

Jacobean times because of her clothes, particularly the lace at her throat.

The Vickers had a sixteen year old son who spent a lot of time in the cottage alone. They decided not to tell him about the 'visitor' so as not to make him uncomfortable in the house. The next year he was at home at Easter. One morning he came down and told his mother he had a strange dream: it was exactly the same experience she had had the previous year.

She told Amanda that no one had ever told them there was a ghost connected with the house, and she had never believed in them. She subsequently heard that there had been sightings of this lady for hundreds of years, and that she had been documented in Lethbridge's books.

19

Bovey Cross

Wyn Clarke: When I worked at the factory (during the war) there was a married woman called Jessy Freeman and she used to walk from the factory to Seaton. This particular night she was walking home, and she got to Bovey Cross ... she saw this ghost stood by the signpost and it frightened her so much she turned around and went all the way back to the village again!

Rita Saunders: There used to be a fir tree at Bovey Cross. I always used to shut my eyes going past ...

20

Lower House

Peggy Tucker tells the following story: ....Harry's (Peggy's husband) great or great-great-uncle Nicholas married Anna Maria Carslake ... they didn't get on and she went and lived where Kelvin lived.* Nicholas presumably stayed on at Lower House... He was a nasty piece of work... The story goes that he walks down the lane with a white horse. He doesn't ride it, he leads it. He leads it through the brown door** and down to the spring and waters it ... The old people would never go down Lower House lane.

* *Kelvin and Phoebe Spencer lived at Wootons.*
** *The brown door leads into the garden of Lower House. It's to the South of the house. The spring is in the garden.*

Rita Saunders: My grandfather, Harry Abbott, lived at Rising Sun, and he used to see Nicholas Ford on the white horse going down towards the brown door at Lower House. Nicholas Ford was Clement Ford's grandfather. He was a ladies' man.

Peggy Tucker recounts another story: When Mark, her grandson, was about five and was staying at Lower House, he was sleeping upstairs. Suddenly there were piercing screams from the bedroom. Celia (Peggy's daughter) rushed up, and he said, 'There's a very nasty man here'. Celia said, 'What does he look like?' and he said, 'I can't tell you except that he's only from the waist up'. You see, in the old house the floors were on a different level ... if this was a ghost walking he would have been walking on a different level from the present floor.

I went to Phoebe Spencer and told her the tale and asked her if she could exorcise him for us. She said, 'Of course I can – I'll try anyway'. She went and she sat there for about an hour and she said, 'Yes, there is something there, a very unhappy man.' And, she said, 'I said to him "Please go away and don't bother us. We don't want you here"'. And we haven't seen anything of him since.

21

Wootons

Peggy Tucker: Phoebe and Kelvin (Spencer) had a friend down to stay and he was the only guest in the house. Phoebe went into the kitchen to prepare the dinner and he went upstairs to change. Presently he came down and went into the sitting room and there was a woman sitting in Phoebe's chair and so he thought at first that it was Phoebe. Then he looked again and saw that it wasn't. He went into the kitchen and said 'Phoebe, who else is in the house, I thought I was the only visitor here?' She said, 'You are'. 'But,' he said, 'there's a woman sitting in your chair.' 'Oh yes,' Phoebe said, 'I know all about her, she's often sitting there.'

49

Another story that Phoebe told. She was in the kitchen and she saw a boy running down the stone steps (outside the window). She described his clothes – he was wearing short trousers and shoes and socks. She expected to hear the bell ring. She went on with what she was doing and she looked up again and there wasn't anybody there. And then she suddenly realised he came down those steps *without making a sound and yet she saw that he was wearing shoes...*

22

Vicarage Hill

Elsie Mayo: This was a dream, but it was so vivid that I hope someone can recognise and verify my ghost!

I heard the sound of a horse's hooves going slowly up the lane, and went to look out of my bedroom window. I knew I must follow up the hill. I then watched as a little wizened coachman climbed down from his seat and stood, holding his long whip, looking back towards the village.

He was dressed in a greeny-black coat with a caped collar, old black breeches and stockings, and shoes with buckles. He wore a tricorn hat.

His coach was a small covered one, ancient and black, as was the horse that stood in the shafts with its head down.

'That's the Dead coach,' someone said, and I was aware that he was waiting for the next death in the village, to take the body away.

He had stopped in the rocky hollow just past what is now the driveway to Hazelwood, but I don't remember the drive being there. Does anyone else know about him?

The Old Vicarage –
which used to be on The Square:
a counterfeit ghost!

Mrs A. Wolsey Harris, Pulman's Weekly News *13 May 1952:*
During the period when smuggling was active, prior to the
formation of the Preventive Service in 1830, places of
concealment were numerous, passages and trapdoors were found
in old vicarages, showing that the vicars were with their
parishioners in the operations of smuggling.*

In Branscombe, after the death of the Vicar's manservant – a
young man who had met with an accident – a report soon
circulated through the village that his ghost had been seen along

51

*Smuggling began about 1770 and ended, as a profitable
business in 1830, with the lowering of import duties.*

the cliffs between Branscombe and Beer where smuggling was going on, especially near the spot where John Harley, the excise officer, had met his death in 1775. The spot was used by the smugglers when getting their tubs of spirit to the top of the cliffs.

One evening when the excise officer was 'on the prowl' he looked through the window of the old Vicarage (which was in the Square). To his intense amazement and horror he saw, seated on either side of the fireplace, the Vicar and the ghost smoking clay pipes and drinking.* The officer watched, fascinated, until the ghost rose from his chair and shook hands with the Vicar. As the ghost turned to the door the officer recognised the ghost as the notorious smuggler of the district, who had donned ghostly clothes to facilitate his smuggling operations.

*Barbara Farquharson: Who was the vicar? Given the dates, the records suggest that it could have been John Anthony Foote 1758- , or John Kingman 1784- , or Thomas Puddicombe 1794- , or Whittington Landon 1827- ...I'd put my money on Puddicombe.

The Old Vicarage, Beach Road

Pam Tickell, as told to Barbara Farquharson: When Marston and Pam Tickell came to the Old Vicarage there were terrible bangings in a small room near the kitchen. It was a room that Pam used for flower arrangement. One morning she came in and found one of her vases lying smashed on the ground. A poltergeist?

Phoebe Spencer said that the last vicar to live there had been a very bad-tempered fellow! After a while, the ghost gave up, and ever since it's been a very peaceful place.

The Field on Beach Road, above the Old Vicarage, opposite Higher Lane

Phoebe Spencer, Sept. 17th 1988: Lady Lloyd's son, Dick, had a car accident. He drove off the road at this point and the friend that was with him was killed. That corner is said to be haunted. The story goes that one of the villagers was coming up from the allotments (Under Hooken fields) with a basket on his back. The basket was tugged and he looked round at his friend and said, 'Don't pull my basket.' The friend said, 'I didn't touch your basket.' It happened again and he looked round and the friend said, 'No, I didn't.' The friend came and walked beside him – and the basket was pulled again. (It's said that) Dick Lloyd saw something in the road which is why he went over the edge...

In another version of the story – told by Margaret Tomlinson – Dick was drunk ...

26

Beach Road down from Higher Lane

Lilly Gush recounted, Sept. 21st 1988, that her father told her: 'Well, I don't know, 'cos I seed some old thing, going along the main Seaside Road (Beach Road), ... down from Higher Lane...' And, Lily said, 'He seed somebody in white and he went in mud pits and father went too'. He says, 'I thought to meself if you be a ghost I'll see what's under the white sheet', and he went till he come to the kiln, somewhere right up the very top somewhere, where they used to dig out lime and he said, "I lost him... I wasn't going in the lime kiln and burn myself", but he didn't know, he always said, "I don't know, can't make out that.."'.

27

Little Seaside

Elsie Mayo: Close to the bridge, at the entrance to the field, I heard a woman crying and crying. There was nobody there.

28

Great Seaside Farm

Mrs E.N. Hughes : Living at Great Seaside Farm in the 1970s was vastly different to to-day. I had visitors who stayed mostly two weeks at a time. We were a friendly farmhouse, and mostly they returned annually.

One evening I was called out as a gate had been left open allowing the cattle on the road. An elderly couple staying with me were very upset because the gentleman who I had left sitting with his wife at the dining table declared that he met a figure when he went upstairs, in black, and she seemed to disappear as he approached her. This unnerved them, and to this day they repeat this episode. They will tell you they were really, really frightened.

On another occasion my friend and her husband were sleeping in the next bedroom to my husband and I. Sitting down to breakfast she declared she had heard someone walking outside her door, and she said 'I heard you last night.' I said, 'You didn't, Jean, because I went to bed, I was so tired, I was absolutely exhausted.'

John and Ida were also frequent visitors and one evening she asked how she should lock the door as they would be late returning. I said just turn the key (it was quite a large old-fashioned one), and that would be sufficient. The next morning she came down and she stood beside the dining table. There were some visitors, and she said 'I want to apologise to the person I locked out last night.' No-one answered, so I said, 'I don't think you locked anyone out, Ida.' So she said, 'I know I did because I heard the footsteps come up the stairs after I got upstairs'. My husband said it must have been our dog, to which she replied they were much heavier than a dog. She said it in very, very plain language.

Then I was sleeping alone in the house and my sons were out, when I thought I heard footsteps on the stairs. I expected my youngest son to shout 'Goodnight Mother', as he always did. Well, I heard these footsteps, and then nothing. I thought, who is that walking in my house? Then the lights flashed in the farm yard and it was my son. He said goodnight and that was that. I said to my husband, 'What a strange thing, there were footsteps up the stairs before Peter came in. I heard them, just like somebody walking upstairs.' My husband said, 'Oh, you're just imagining things.' But you don't imagine it, it is very, very plain.

To sum up, the footsteps were heard, I know, for three years running by different people. Of course when you have storms the wind blows through the thatch and all that, and it's terribly, terribly eerie. I just don't know, I can't say what it was. I wasn't nervous, but I must admit I would have liked to have gotten to the bottom of it. My husband said, 'For goodness sake don't broadcast that we've got things walking around the house or we won't have any visitors come at all'.

After my husband died, on the backstairs, I did think there was a figure went that way. In fact I did go up to look, but there was nothing.

At the farm there was supposed to have been someone who hung themselves in the cider press and some people think it all comes from that. But that didn't worry me, it was the footsteps.

Lilly Gush, 1988: Farmer Charlie (Perryman) was a nice young man, he committed suicide. I don't wonder, because I don't think he married the one he liked most and they had a kid and he had a funny head, water on the brain, and he died, and it wasn't long after that when he hanged hiself from a tree. Oh dear, dear.

29

The A 3502 from Sidmouth to Lyme Regis

Margaret Tomlinson in Three Generations in the Honiton Lace Trade, *pp 21-22:* (Abigail Chick died in 1859. She was a strong-minded early lace trader who lived at Berry Barton. She loved animals and believed that in her after-life she would see her own favourite grey pony once more). Half a century after Abigail's death her great grand-daughter, Elsie Chick, then a girl of twenty, had a curious experience...Elsie and her two younger sisters were returning in the family donkey-cart from an expedition to Sidmouth...Dusk was falling and the girls, driving along the main road, were uncertain which of the many turnings to Branscombe was the correct route for home. As they approached the second or third turning they saw, coming towards them along the main road, a lady riding side-saddle on a white horse. Before they could stop to ask the way she turned down the lane to Branscombe. Elsie hastily climbed down from the cart and followed her, but a bend in the road blocked the view. Hurrying around it, Elsie saw a straight stretch ahead, but the lady and the horse were nowhere to be seen. Somewhat surprised, she returned to the donkey-cart and almost at once a man with a bridle in his hand came towards the girls along the main road. He asked if they had seen anything of his runaway horse, but when they replied that all they had seen was a white horse with a woman riding on it, he swore under his breath and passed on... Talking the matter over (the girls) agreed that no sound had been heard from the hooves of the white horse. Some twelve years later, during the First World War, Elsie was attending a working party in Sidmouth and happened to mention that she was staying in Branscombe. Someone then asked her if she had ever seen the Branscombe ghost – a woman who rode along the main road on a white horse. In after years Elsie half believed that the apparition she had seen was Abigail herself, making her way home to Berry Barton. Could the white horse then have been the beloved grey pony, reunited at last with its mistress?

Thomas Charles Lethbridge*

Tom and Mina Lethbridge came to live at Hole House in Branscombe in 1957. Tom died in 1971, and his wife left the village.

Tom was a Cambridge-trained archaeologist, and, for thirty years, he was keeper of the Anglo-Saxon Antiquities at the University Museum. But, as time went on, he became more and more interested in para-psychology. Some people consider him 'The Einstein of the paranormal'. Others think he's off the wall...

Lethbridge was particularly interested in ghosts and divining. He thought, as Peter Underwood put it, 'that the dowser and the ghost hunter should walk hand in hand'. He also had ideas about life after death, poltergeists, magic, second sight, precognition and the nature of time.

He wrote at least eight books: **Gogmagog, The Buried Gods, Witches, Investigating an Ancient Religion, Ghost and Ghoul, Ghosts and Divining Rod** and **The Power of the Pendulum.**

In many of them he explored the theory that a variety of field forces connected woods and water, hills and open areas, and that, to quote Michael Williams, 'Nature (was) packed with strange tape recordings, dating back thousands and thousands of calendars'. He believed that people could enter into, or leave, 'fields' of depression that were imprinted, often in watery or humid places, either from the past or the future. Just as underground water exerts a magnetic field that can be picked up with a dowsing rod, so, he suggested, water could record and transmit strong emotions. And so too with ghosts. The woman who appeared to Lethbridge near to the mill (p. 37) was standing directly above an underground stream (which he was able to locate with his dowsing rod). As Colin Wilson put it:'(She) was almost certainly just another 'tape recording' − a kind of

videotape recording this time...', and the forcefield could as easily have recorded pleasant or elated emotions as unhappy ones.

You, the reader, may accept, or not accept, Lethbridge's findings. He also believed – and here the reader may have more trouble following – in the power of the pendulum. At given lengths (always measured in inches – because they were 'natural' measurements, based on the human body!) it would gyrate to different substances – glass, lead, iron, amber, even garlic, apples, alcohol and truffles – and also to different colours and emotions...

61

Tom Lethbridge and Charlie Cox.

Lethbridge believed that there are other realms of reality beyond our world, and that there are forms of energy that we do not even begin to understand. Do you?

These notes are extracted from Colin Wilson's The Unexplained (Orbis Press 1984), *and Michael Williams'* Phenomena of the West (Bossiney Books 1994) *courtesy of Steven Shipp of Sidmouth.*